MOVING US OUT

America's Dark History of Redlining and Gentrifying Black Communities

Rashaad Singleton

Prelude

This book was written to make Black people worldwide understand the silent war that is being waged on them. Through redlining and gentrification, millions of black families have been displaced by people who value profit over humanity. The time for that to end ....is now.

Dedication

This book is dedicated to the kids in rural cities and the children in rural towns. Don't give up and never give in.

Table of Contents

They're Moving Us Out

Chapter 1: The "Hood" Was Created

There's a typical question that white America loves to ask each other, "Why can't black people get it together?" They love to bring up our housing conditions in the urban cities, as if we were not place there strategically. They like to discuss issues of black on black crime as if that was not also orchestrated at the highest levels of government. Their audacity to only see the result of a crisis and not the cause of that crisis is indeed staggering; but that's just it isn't it? Of course, they can see what's being done. They are the ones that's doing it after all. Who are benefiting from over-packed communities with poor education and poor health care? The answer is obvious. They don't want to discuss the root of our problems, because usually that's a path that will lead directly to them.

The "Hood," as we like to call it, was not some natural event that occurred in our communities. Absolutely not. The hood was and is designed methodically by white supremacy. That's why there is a liquor store on every corner, that's why it's a fast food restaurant on every block, and more importantly, that's why it's hardly little to no good jobs near our communities. The hood for white America is a cash cow. Why? Because black people do not practice group economics and the black dollar doesn't bounce one time in our communities. However, it bounces 7 times in the white community, 18 times in the Asian community, and 21 times in the so-called Jewish community. We must fix this family. "Practicing group economics" has to be more than a cool, woke saying to put on a T-Shirt. It has to be a way of life and make no doubt about it, our futures do depend on it. If our communities are gentrified by people outside of our communities, how will we be able master group economics? We should be buying up every piece of commercial property that we can, so that we can put black businesses in those properties and practice group economics every day and not just some days.

When we buy up the hood and youth see black business owners from a young age that will positively impact their lives a great deal. When a black child sees a black business owner, he or she also feels that they can become a business owner also. Representation is key and this should be the norm in any black society. Yet, that is not the reality for many black communities. A lot of our people don't have access to healthy food choices. Many can't find good work and therefore, they drink alcohol or turn to drugs to escape their pain for a little while.

So when you have bad food choices that's owned by white people, an abundance of liquor stores that's owned by white people, whose products are owned by white people, and no good jobs available, how is that black community supposed to create a positive impact?

Then there's the combination of drugs and guns. Do you know any black-owned gun companies? Because the author doesn't. Did black people own planes in the 60's to fly pure Colombian coke in black communities? Of course not. All of these things were strategically placed in our communities by white supremacy hiding behind government titles in the hopes that we would self-destruct. They failed. We are still here damm it....

Master psychiatrist, Amos Wilson, says that's there are two types of criminals, white - collar criminals and blue-collar criminals. He said white criminals have the ability to do their illegal activities in skyscrapers buildings so the world does not see them clearly for the crooks that they are. Whereas black crimes are more confrontational because of the close proximity of the people within the community. Therefore, they try to propagate us as "criminals" when they are biggest thieves in the history of the world as the stealing of a nation and the stealing of a people bears witness. It is very common behavior for criminals to point the finger at other people and call them criminals. "I didn't invent the hood although I created redlining and racial steering." "I have nothing to do with black on black crime, although I flooded your neighborhoods with drugs and guns." This is the sound of white denial.

It's very simple to understand. If you take a box and you put some dogs in there and you drop a little piece of food in there everyday, after a while, the dogs are going to get tired. Their patience will grow thin and soon, they will become violent for that little piece of food that's being dropped in the box. He or she will be over aggressive and might even kill the other dogs just to get that piece of food.

However the question remains. Who is giving that little piece food, knowing that it is not enough? And who placed all these damn dogs in small box to begin with?

This is what we are faced with in black America. We love to say we have a crab in barrels complex, but crabs don't belong in a barrel. So who put the barrel there?

Chapter 2: New Deal

On October 29, 1929, America was struck with The Great Depression. The stock market crashed and banks across the nation closed. Millions of Americans became poor overnight. No matter your race, it was a struggle just to get a hot meal and a warm bed. All Americans were facing problems, and the biggest problem was housing. People were losing their homes every day during the depression because jobs were closing. You think the mortgages stop just because it was a national depression? Absolutely not. White folks still wanted their money and they wanted it on time. Many Americans became instantly homeless because of the fact that they were living pay check to pay check. For the first time, white America had a little taste of what it was like to be black and have all your profits taken from you without notice. They could now understand what it was like when your government fail you. This lasted until 1939 after a plan was put together to help save families across the nation...white families that is.

The 32nd President of the United States, Franklin D. Roosevelt had an answer for the problems that was facing white America. He introduced the New Deal in 1933. It was a series of programs, public work projects, financial reforms, and regulations to help white families get back on their feet.

Now although America loves to paint some type of heavenly light on Franklin D. Roosevelt, he was a hardcore segregationist. When the New Deal started, public housing was to be offered to white families only, all across America in the hope of helping them recover from the Great Depression. Now, Roosevelt built some housing projects for African Americans as well, but they were not nearly as luxurious or modern as the "white only" buildings and the properties was completely separate from each other.

As time went on, white tenants begin to leave public housing because banks were offering them loans will little money down to get houses in the suburbs. On the contrary, in black public housing, it was so full, that people were being put on waiting lists and most were on the waiting list for extremely long periods of time. The white public housing became so vacant that that the owners begin to lose money. They had no choice, but to integrate for the sake of financial gain, not love and humility.

Well, here is where it got tricky. As thousands of black families began to move to the housing projects in urban cites, white industries was methodically moving their industries from those cities. Now black people were trapped. Just like herding cattle inside a closed fence, they had us right where they wanted us. They wanted us to live on top on each other with no economic flow. The only source of money that is constantly flowing in any community is crime, which is exactly what white America needed to fuel the systemic mass incarceration that we know today. They designed the hood to be a prisoner-making machine using black people as the nuclear core.

What is truly painful is when black people did get on their feet and were eventually ready to leave their housing projects, their troubles were just beginning. They had another hurdle waiting for them, the Federal Housing Administration, also known as FHA. The FHA, like the New Deal was also founded by President Franklin D. Roosevelt. The FHA has the authority to control the construction and underwriting for properties. They also protect loans made by banks and other private lenders for housing developments. The main purpose of this institution is to stabilize the mortgage market and to provide comfortable housing and good living conditions for the population. Well, although that that might sound good, all of those positive things were for white folks only.

When black people would try to seek proper housing for their families, they were shown just how nasty some white folks can be. The FHA underwriters told banks that no loans were to be issued to black families. That's why the author hates colorism, because in those days, it didn't matter if you were light-skin, brown-skin, or dark-skin. If you were black, you were quickly told "no." They promoted the idea that if one black family entered a white community, the property value would immediately go down. This was false of course, as many black families were paying double the amount of white people to live in certain white communities in order to escape the slums of the inner-cites. These racist guidelines were adopted quickly by private industry. The United States government personally gave white private citizens the tools and the power to act on their racism. Housing Unit developers would put up big signs, "negroes need not apply" or "exclusive families only."

The FHA created colored maps. Based on the rating of your community, you would receive a specific color that was to show if your neighborhood was a good place to issue loans. Green was "best," blue was "still desirable," yellow was "definitely declining," and red was "hazardous." If you lived in an all-white community and you were nowhere near black people, you received a green color. If you were in a black community or a white community that had black people moving in, that community would receive a red color and was less likely to get a loan. This practice of marking black communities "red" became known as "redlining." Please note, not only did they want to issue loans to only all white communities, they wanted to issue loans to all white communities that were far from away black people. Once again, that is the government training and conditioning white people to think racist and to live racist. All of the good mortgages went to white America in the suburbs. Black people as always, were left out. This racist legislation help fueled the racist whites of America and promoted the idea that having black people in your communities was the worst thing in the world.

Desperate measures was taken in some white communities to make sure that they received a positive FHA rating. We will speak in later chapters on how white people built walls to separate themselves from their black neighbors in order to get a positive FHA rating. They would later become even more sophisticated and instead of building walls, they would just simply build highways and inter-states through our communities. By building interstates through black communities, they hope to keep black people on one side of the road and white people on other.

Between 1934 and 1962, the federal of government gave over 120 billion dollars for new housing developments. Out of 120 billion dollars, only 2% was issued to non-whites.

Chapter 3: Wealth

There is hidden knowledge about wealth that is passed down from generation to generation in white families. They don't talk about it with us out of fear that they will lose their control. For example, any adult will tell you that owning your own home is the key to acquiring wealth. If you own a home, you have the value of the property and you also have the equity that comes with it. Well damn, shouldn't this be emphasized in grade school? It seems to the author, that we should be learning less about dinosaurs and more about acquiring wealth. So there's the first offense, it's not taught in schools. Here's the 2nd offense, most of our white friends who also know this knowledge do not share it with us either. This is their way of staying on code. It's just some things many white folks won't openly discuss with black people, no matter how close a friend you think you are. This is because even some of the nicest white people are very comfortable knowing that white people are in power. If they were your friends, they would tell you about how their ancestors were able to receive loans that black people never got the chance to receive and they would tell you about how they stole the land. Usually, it's quite the opposite. Damn, nearly every white person in America feels as if they did not benefit from slavery, Jim Crow, and housing discrimination. If you let them tell it, they all had to start from the ground up. However, when you understand redlining and gentrification and how it's displacing black families for the specific purpose of building white wealth, you can clearly see that the only people who think white people start from the ground up, is white people.

Certain things become clear. This is why they didn't not want us to own homes and they did not want us to acquire wealth. White people did not want us to catch up to them and we most definitely would have if we were offered the same housing loans as them. Instead of thousands of dollars in loans, we got thousands of dollars in debt. From the 1930 to the 1970's, white people were given loans left and right. If they lived in area with no black people, they practically gave you the home. What do they do now in 2019? Those same properties that was basically given to white people and denied to black people are being sold for millions! Because of pure racism in the form of redlining and gentrification in the 1950's and 60's, white people are now allowed to profit millions of dollars from these investments while at the same time saying, "I did not benefit from the exploitation of black people." On top of that, most will only sell to other white people, in hopes of keeping that community as white as possible. They then use the profit gained from selling those homes to gentrify black communities. Now white people own that previous property and they are coming to own ours also. Rent is raised and products become more expensive, but the job opportunities do not change. We are forced to move out, but damn, where are we supposed to go? Once you begin to riddle this question, their end goal for black people becomes obvious. They wish to make us obsolete.

There's a feeling that comes with owning a property. One is able to be comfortable in their privacy. They always have the ability to rent their home out and make extra money. They can grow crops and literally make money come out of the ground. White people constructed American society very carefully so that they alone could enjoy the simple freedoms of financial stability....and that is demonic. Many white students get the nice cars when they are only 16 years old and many black kids have to wait much later. Why? That's directly connected to the equity that was built over decades through racist legislation. It's simply equity built off racism. They use this equity to purchase whatever they want. Many of these homes who were only offered to white families are passed down from generation to generation with each family member benefiting from the prejudice guideline such as "redlining."

By pushing black people in low-income housing and then removing the job industries from the community, black people were totally left out of decades of wealth development. White folks were pulling us around like strings. You would think it would stop there, but when one is forced to live in an apartment building, they are at the mercy of the landlord. If they want to raise the rent, they can raise the rent. If they want to sell building, they can sell the building. This can be nerve reckoning for a tenant and that's exactly what white American wanted black America to feel, constant unease.

Hundreds of thousands of dollars are made from being a home owner. At the same time, the property acquires hundreds of thousands of dollars in equity. Family, it has to be understood, none of that money is being made in the renting process. I repeat, none of that money is made in the renting process. Many people have a business within their homes, such as dog watching or doing hair. You think the landlord is going to allow you to have a business inside of his building for free? Absolutely not. The landlord controls your housing and your potential business income by simply not allowing you have to have a business in the building. That's one stream of income that's immediately erased just by simply not having your own home. Instead of getting thousands of dollars in business profit, most black America's are giving thousands of dollars in rent. That's is the main problem in the wealth division between black America and white America. White America to this day, is profiting from racist housing regulations that the federal government wrote up themselves. Redlining and other racist regulations ensure that wealth would stay inside of white families for generations to come. They wanted to force us into being a nation of tenants and not homeowners, because they know owning your own home is the key to building wealth. They made it so that their housing would later makes them rich, while our housing made landlords rich. As usual, they always find a way to profit off our survival.

Chapter 4: Education

There's an old saying, "yea it's good, but at what cost?" Many black Americans wanted to believe in the American dream. The idea of living next to decent people despite race or religion seemed like a great idea to black folks. After the Civil Rights Act was passed in 1964, black people could finally go to the same schools that white people went to. People who had been conditioned to hate us their whole lives were now in full control of our education.

No longer would we learn about the beautiful black history that our grandparents were accustomed to. We would be told Columbus discovered America and presidents who were slave owners like Columbus should be admired as great men and heroes of their time. At the same time, black children could enter white schools finally; real history and knowledge of self became pretty much obsolete.

The education was just one aspect of it. What about lunch time? In the classroom, white teachers trained you how to think white, but it would be the cafeteria where children would learn how to shop white. How many products by black-owned businesses were sold during your lunch in school? Think about that for a minute. Any chips? Any drinks? Any candy? Or were they all white, like the majority of schools in America? Yes, we were conditioned to think like white people and then were conditioned to spend our money with white people. Then we wonder what's wrong? What's wrong is that since 1st grade, we have been programmed to be consumers and not producers. The education in the classroom won't teach that and the people who are in control of the cafeteria food won't expose that. If there were black-owned options in the cafeteria, wouldn't that by default teach black children and white children that shopping for black-owned products is just as important as shopping for white-owned products. Instead of that healthy balanced knowledge, Black children are consequently taught to spend all of their money on white businesses, while white folks don't have to spend a nickel on black businesses. We learn all that, just from going to school lunch.

Places that America used to consider ghettos are now being bought up and gentrified for profit. It used to be that black people were desperate to get into white communities, now days white people are desperate to get into black communities. So what happens when white people begin to move into a black community? They want the black people there to move out. They don't say it verbally. No, instead they raise mortgages and monthly rent. That is there passive way of saying, "black people leave." If you own a building and the property value goes up, you're winning. If you are renting, which is the reality for most black Americans in urban cities, life becomes a disaster. The city that you belonged to your whole life instantly becomes too expensive to live, by just the arrival of people who care more about profit than community. Some may say that because property value goes up, that's good for the community because now they will get more resources. Resources intended for who? They build private schools and make enrollment so expensive, that the majority of black people won't be able to attend. For those who can pay the amount, there is still an interview process that even rich black children can be weeded out of. Then they make housing so expensive, that black people can't afford to live in it. Better housing, better education, and better facilities should not be dependent on how many white people live in that community. It shouldn't take the arrival of white folks to improve the society in black communities, those conditions should already be established beforehand, to all tax paying citizens.

Why do we have to wait for white kids to go to our schools to get nice computers for our children? Why do we have to wait for white families to move into our communities for the streets to be clean? That is a clear indication that financial fundings will only be allowed to us if we give up territory to white people. Colonization by the name of gentrification.

Chapter 5: Portland

The author spent summers in Portland as a child. The white people there always seemed to be extra friendly and cheerful to the point where it was distinguishable from other white Americans. Yet, there is something that's obvious in Portland. The black population is low...very low...and nobody wants to talk about it. Could it be that white people in Oregon might be extra friendly because they are trying to cover up a dark past?

Many people are not aware of this, but The City of Roses, also known as Portland, was once known as the most racist city outside of the south. It started with Oregon's Black Exclusion Laws. The first was written 1844 when the Provisional Government of Oregon forced all black people to leave the state. Each black person that was found living in the state after the law passed was to be whipped "not less than twenty nor more than thirty-nine stripes" every 6 months. So much for friendly white people right? These laws would be in effect until the 1920's. That's almost 100 years that white people had to cut Oregon up for themselves. As always, when they finally owned everything and all the land, then they allowed black people to come in to work the land. In some instances, black people had to be out of town by sundown. If not, there lives could be in danger by white supremacy. Beating and even lynching would occur if black people were caught at the wrong time in the wrong city. These towns that practiced this inhumane treatment become known as Sundown Towns. Signs and posters would be put up high for all to see, warning black people that they had better get out of town before dark.

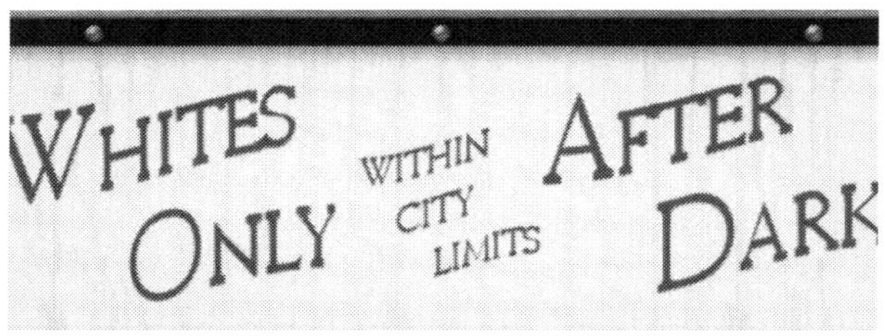

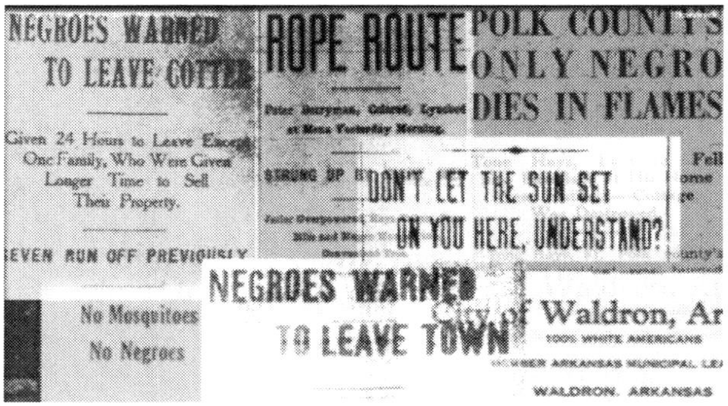

Understand, there was only so many roads back in those days. Imagine the trauma and horror you had if your car broke in the middle of the night in one of these towns. Imagine if you had your family in the car with you and you started having engine problems. This is the reality that our ancestors had to endure just to live in the country that they had been born in.

This led to the development of "The Green Book," which is a guidebook for black road trippers. The guide was made by New York mailman, Victor Hugo Green. "The Green Book" explained specific details about where black people should and should not navigate. "The Green Book" was responsible for protecting millions of black lives from white supremacy in sundown times.

After World War II, black military men came home hoping to feel like heroes, but there would be no "welcome home" signs in Portland. Instead of "welcome home" signs, black service members were met with signs that read "we don't serve to blacks," and "blacks need not apply." Military or not, black people could not own land and black people could not own property. Skilled black engineers in the military could barely get work as a janitor in Portland, Oregon. After serving their country faithfully, they were still being treated like 2nd class citizens. Worst, those bigots were treating black people like dogs. They would not even let a thirsty black child buy a cold drink. So, never-mind Mississippi and Alabama as historically being two of the most prejudice states, Oregon sets its own bar with it came to racism, gentrification and segregation. In 1920, there were 250,000 people in Portland. For every black person, there were 150 white people. Without question, Portland became one of the whitest cities in America, due to its use of black exclusion laws.

In 1922, the KKK elected a governor and a mayor who handpicked the chief of police. As depicted below.

CHIEF KLUXERS TELL LAW ENFORCEMENT OFFICERS JUST WHAT MYSTIC ORGANIZATION PROPOSES TO DO IN CITY OF PORTLAND

Today Portland is gentrified daily and black people are still being pushed out of their communities. It is not by chance or circumstance. It is and has always been highly orchestrated and it's being hidden behind warm smiles and cheerful greetings.

Chapter 6: Detroit

One thing needs to be clear. White people didn't just start building walls when Trump became president. White people have been building walls and they were not trying to keep out just Mexicans out, they were specifically trying to keep black people out. In 1941, The Wall of Detroit was built because the federal government was only going to insure loans to white people, if they could prove without a shadow of a doubt that their community would stay strictly white. When the white citizens of 8-mile were denied housing loans, they built a 6 foot wall separating themselves from their black neighbors. The black residents said that the wall made the area feel like 2 separate countries. When the walls went up, the loans came down. Black Americans were being controlled by racism in the form of real estate. There was nothing black people could do about it except stay in their improvised communities. By building a wall and receiving home loans, the federal government gave a clear signal that they would reward white people for acting out on their racism. The government was conditioning white people to be racist and most didn't even know it. Years later, those same white folks who got new homes for little money down would sell them for 5 times their worth. Because of this, black people were denied generations of wealth accumulation. It would not change until the Federal Housing Act passed in 1968, but the damage had already been done. For almost 30 years, white people got all of the new modern homes exclusively, while black people were left to figure it out in the slums.

Today in Detroit, racism is as strong as it's ever been, although they are not as direct as they used to be. Instead of saying "no blacks allowed," they have mastered "racially steering." This is a practice that real estate agents use in order to prevent someone of color from getting a home of their choice. You may have your heart set on getting a nice home in Detroit, but based on the community, if it's all white, a realtor can easily say, "no." They will instead, try persuade that person of color to move to the black side of town or an area with less financial backing. Everyday black people are being racially steered and don't even know it. One way to check if you are being racially steered is to have a white person that has similar qualifications as you and have them go and apply for the same property as you. If they are treated differently than you, then you know you have been racially steered.

There are other problems such as the expansions of schools and businesses. As they expand, the rent increases in the area. In some cases they just raise the rent every 6 months until you can't afford to live there anymore. There's no communication with the community, it's just rich white folks being rich white folks at the expense of black people. As they gather wealth, thousands of black families and Hispanic families are rendered homeless.

Chapter 7: Baltimore

When the government cannot persuade you to move off your land, they can force you to leave. This process is called "eminent domain." The definition of eminent domain is the right of a government or its agent to expropriate private property for public use, with payment of compensation. In Baltimore, Maryland, black people are very familiar with this injustice. Although many people praise hospitals for saving people lives, one often forgets that they are still a business, and when it comes to real estate they can be some of the biggest sharks in the community. Such is the case with John Hopkins Hospital in Middle East, Baltimore. Where many black families used to live, it is all hospital property now. Thousands of black family homes were ceased by the federal government so that white folks could expand their hospital, but it gets even more interesting. White politicians are personal friends with the owners of these hospitals and other big corporations. They are the ones approving this. So you have city elected officials that are making public/private partnerships in order to make their own pockets fat. Who suffers? Black folks. Black people are forced to leave their homes no matter what, just because some white people whom they have never met, just struck a business deal behind closed doors. First, they make black people leave their homes, then they knock down their homes, and then they let their white buddies expand their businesses. Not only do these crooked politicians approve of black homes to be taken, they also give millions of dollars to other white businesses to come in that community to build their projects. It doesn't stop there.

When these new white businesses come into the community after they have essentially stolen land, do you think they hire the black people in that community? Hell no. Businesses bring in their own people and construction companies bring in their own crew. Black people are left to watch their community get taken over. These white companies pay their workers decent salaries as well, which allows them to pay more rent than the average black person who is there. Well, those workers don't want to travel to the suburbs, they want to live closer to their job. As they move into black communities, rent rises, products and services become more expensive, but the job opportunities for black people does not change. Slowly, but surely, black people are forced to move out. This begins the final stage of gentrification. The complete erasing of a people, and it happens through the alliances of politicians and businessmen making public/private partnerships.

Most residents of Baltimore agree that there needed to be some drastic improvements in the community. When dealing with gentrification, it's not that people don't want better housing and public facilities. They are not against redevelopment, they just wanted to be a part of it. The problem with gentrification is not allowing the citizens within that community to participate, but instead giving them a few crumbs to move out. When companies do that and politicians allow them to do that, it becomes quite clear that the redevelopment taking place is not a redevelopment for black people, but it's a redevelopment for white people and a removing of black people. Many black people in Baltimore were not given the option to stay in their home or not, they were told to leave. The CEOs of these companies that are going inside these black communities should be asking people if they want to stay or if they want to go. Instead, they are sending text messages from their private yachts that read, "have the blacks left yet?" No compassion. No humanity, just greed. Greed, greed, greed.

Gentrification can be subtle. It can be racism right in your face and you won't even realize it. For example, when gentrification is being taking place in a black community, you will see a significant rise in price on everyday items. This is somewhat code, "for no blacks allowed." In Baltimore, around many gentrified communities, signs are put up that read, "no food stamps allowed." Now why would a company put a sign that bans a major currency that used black people within that community? Because they are clearly saying once again, "no blacks allowed."

How do we combat it? We must unite. We must form local organizations and identify black investors in the area to buy up our communities before they do.

Chapter 8: New York

When you ask the average foreigner which city would they like to visit in America, 9/10 they will always say New York City. From Brooklyn to Harlem, New York is full of culture and traditions. The black community is a big part of the identity of New York and always have been. What's beginning to change that is gentrification. For years, black people have begged city officials for better public schools and affordable housing. White New Yorkers made only a few private schools and enrolled mostly white children. In private schools, each child has to be interviewed and "accepted" in that school. Many black children who fit the criteria that is needed are turned away simply because they are black. However. it's almost impossible to prove that as the decisions of enrollment is completely at the owner's discretion. Once again, this is one of their subtle ways of saying, "no blacks allowed." So after that, that black child may be forced to go to a public school where little to no funds are being offered. They are literally "trying" to give white children a better education than black children. Well, as white communities begin to grow and expand into black communities, obvious changes begin to occur. The trash is picked up more regularly and the schools become safer and more modern. Why do we have to wait for arrival of white people for our schools to get better? We pay taxes just like everyone else. For years, Hollywood profited off telling the story of our dysfunctional schools in our urban communities. They always made it seem like they were some type of maximum security prisons. They always showed them underfunded with disobedient and disrespectful children. However, they did not show the white people withholding money from those schools. Hollywood didn't show us white people strategically withholding money from black communities in order to make that community unsafe. No, mainstream media just focused on the results of withholding funds and services, they never discussed the cause. Why do we have to wait for the arrival of white people to get better police protection? Why do we have to wait on white people get better public facilities? The answer is clear. America is just racist as it's ever been, and they do not want us to live comfortably, but rather in despair.

With gentrification comes the subtle racism. In Brooklyn, Harlem, and other black communities, white people are moving in and straight up calling the police on them. No questions asked. Their thought process is, "You're black, I never seen you before, I'm calling the police." You can just look unfamiliar or you can just have your music too loud and they're calling the police. The culture in New York is loud and upbeat and it has been for centuries. New white people who move to black communities are calling the police on black people that have been living there through 5 generations. This is white privilege at its finest. They seriously think they can dictate how a community will run everywhere they go. This called "Christopher Columbus syndrome."

Because of the gentrification in New York, black people have being experiencing reverse migration. Many families moved north in the early 1900's seeking jobs outside of plantation work. Well now, because of gentrification directly, that is happening in reverse and now many black New Yorkers are moving south for cheaper cost of living. That is inevitable when the rent is raised every 6 months and jobs become scarcer. What doesn't help is the new companies that move in don't hire the black people that are being displaced. No, they bring in their own employees and these employees want to live close to their job....

When one takes a step back and look at the grand scale of things, it is very easy to understand gentrification. You just have to realize who is profiting from it and who is getting displaced by it. It is not fair that the black people who built Bestie are being pushed out of Bestie.

It's not fair that the black people who built Brooklyn are being pushed out of Brooklyn and it damn sure isn't fair that the beautiful black people who built magnificent Harlem are being pushed out of Harlem. The majority of black people are not against white people moving in their community. What is not appreciated is the sense of entitlement that comes with it and the audacity to try to tell black people where they can and cannot go. White people, we are not damn cattle. You can't move us to from one side of the field to the other just because you feel like it. We are the Kings and Queens of this earth and it's high-time that we reminded them of that. If we are to call ourselves Kings and Queens, then we might as well start building our kingdoms right in the heart of our black communities first, before someone else tries to do it. If there is development in a black community that's displacing black people from good health care, good housing and good jobs, that is a development that weaponizing gentrification for the bidding of white supremacy.

Chapter 9: Miami

When one travels to the south beach today, they are completely overwhelmed with positive energy and the good vibes of Miami. The beaches combined with beautiful people make Miami one of the most popular tourist attractions in the world. Tons of different restaurants serving a multitude of people from different cultures and backgrounds, make Miami a non-stop music festival. However, not too long ago, black people were not even allowed in some parts in Miami. Similar to Detroit, Miami had a wall of their own and they didn't allow black people to cross it.

Miami was one of the main cities that practiced redlining. Black people who made just as much money as white people, were not given loans for houses. This was an economic genocide for Black America. White Floridians were allowed to get great properties for little money down. Now today, those properties are worth millions. A white person can know all of this and still look you right in the face and say they didn't benefit from the abuse of black people. The proof is in the pudding. Redlining, being supported by the New Deal and the federal government, made sure black people were left in the slums of Miami instead of being allowed to move into the suburbs.

In Miami, Black people were not allowed to enter white communities at all prior to civil rights. White communities were considered high society back then, no matter how rich or poor they were. Black people were not even allowed to enjoy the beaches. In fact, in order to work on the beach, black people had to have a green card and health card on them at all times.

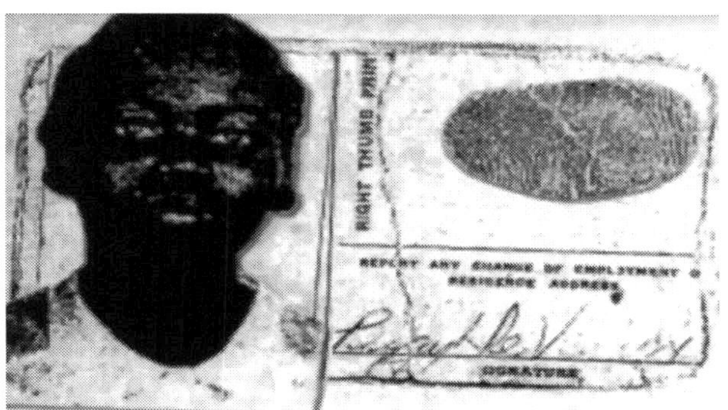

(White supremacy will sometimes be sly about their racism. They won't just say, "no black people allowed." They will often time instead just make you do double the paperwork in hopes of discouraging you. Many black people get frustrated with this process, but many also prevail through it anyway.)

On 62nd Street on 12 Avenue, white people in Miami built a wall that was named "The Wall." Black people were not allowed passed that point. If they were caught behind that wall at night, their very lives could be in danger of being killed by white people. They tore most of the wall down, but there is still a little part of it that is still standing today as a reminder....

They tore down walls, but that does not stop the gentrification. To white land developers, the walls were simply in the way. Instead of walls today, they just raise the rent in Miami so ridiculously high, that it makes it almost impossible for the black people there to stay and it discourages new black people from moving in. Now people that have lived in Miami all their lives can barely afford to live there. Liberty City and little Haiti are the most affected by this. People are coming to black communities and buying up their apartment buildings. These people do not care about the buildings, they just want the space. You don't think nothing about it, and then you get a letter in the mail saying that your rent is being raised 200 dollars. Then boom, it hits you like a ton of bricks. Single parents who are paying 1500 dollars for rent are instantly paying 1700 dollars for rent. This is the most subtle way of saying "I want these blacks out of here."

Yes, behind the sweet mojitos and tall long islands lies a dark past in Miami and the gentrification that's being done today to black communities is being completely ignored. It's all being hidden behind bright lights and loud parties. Meanwhile, black residents are being pushed out every day.

Chapter 10: Chicago

Once the author was educating a white college friend of his. The white friend asked "why do you always talk about what white people are doing to black people, why don't you talk about black on black crime, like in the cities of Chicago?" Typical isn't it? Although the author considered his friend to be a smart guy, he had just exposed his ignorance. There is no question about it, the root of black on black crime is white on black crime. It started with the Chicago Race Riot of 1919? White people killed an innocent black youth by the name of Eugene Williams simply for drifting on the white side of the beach. After that, they burned down hundreds of homes and businesses and left thousands and thousands of black people homeless. What would those communities be if they were not burned down by white supremacy? No reparations were paid, just dry apologies from old politicians that don't give a damn.

Between 1916 and 1920, over 50 thousand black southerners fled to Chicago in hopes of finding work in the industrial sector. White people feared these skilled black labors. So they did what they do best. They terrorized the black community both physically and through legislation. As the black population was increasing, laws were written up that prevented black people from buying and selling land in the best parts of Chicago. Similar to Oregon's Exclusion Laws, black people were not allowed to use the land to build any kind of wealth whatsoever. The federal government had kept us in a position of servitude for centuries, and they were doing their best to try to keep us there. When a black family did eventually save enough money to move in to a comfortable home in Chicago, they would be fire-balled by the local white residents. People would literally throw bombs in their homes just to keep their communities white.

Have we allowed Michael Jordan and the success of the Chicago Bulls make us forget the nasty history of Chicago? Probably so. What happens to all of those displaced black people whose entire lives were destroyed by white supremacy? They were funneled into public housing. Which sooner than later, would become known as the hood, due to the lack of jobs and economic resources. White people created the hood. They created it by burning our homes and forcing us into over packed neighborhoods. They created it by pushing drugs through federal agencies in our communities. They created the hood by dropping off boxes of assault weapons in our communities hoping that we would destroy ourselves.

Now we see the results of it today. We can't not unite because we can barely trust one another. This family is beefing with this family and this gang is fighting with that gang. Do we not see the system that is profiting from all of this destruction? If the people are getting shot all the time, the hospitals are getting paid all the time and the prison system is getting paid at the same time. Who owns the hospitals? Who owns the jails? We must always remember to follow the money. On another note, it is proven that there are more hospitals in white communities in Chicago than black communities. That is a clear indication to black people that the state really cares about the health of white people. However, which side of town is being riddled with bullets? In an emergency, if hospitals are completely filled and a person has to leave their side of town to go to the other of side town for medical treatment, doesn't that decrease their chance of survival? Well, who is behind the system that's housing black people away from hospitals? White supremacy. The proof is plain as day.

Chapter 11: Criminal Justice

So there you have it. For decades, and across cities in America, white supremacy has destroyed black communities and then pushed them into public housing. You would think folks would be able to get some peace after all that hell that they had to endure; however, white supremacy has no limits. After using redlining to isolate us, they begin to flood our neighborhoods with drugs and guns. Then all of the job industries that had once recruited black people from the south purposely left in order to leave black people in overcrowded, jobless, abandoned communities. Then came the police.

We have to understand there was not much police presence in some urban neighborhoods back in the day. So that was sometimes good and sometimes bad depending on if you were dealing with a harassing police department. If you were in bad neighborhood, there might not have been much of a police presence, which in turn, allowed many communities to become unsafe. Now there is a strong police presence in the black community, but it's not used the same way as it is in white communities. It seems that the police exist to protect and serve the white communities, but they also exist to police black people. Yes, quite different from "protect and serve," black people are being policed. The prison population number overwhelmingly agrees to that. Through gentrification, over-crowded black communities are bound to happen, since that is exactly what white land developers and white real estate agents want. They are racially steering black people to live stacked up on each other. Then there is a system that's pumping drugs and weapons in that overcrowded community. Rumors of war begin to spread amongst gangs and many of the rumors are initiated by the government. For the purpose of what? White supremacy wants to turn that black neighborhood into a prisoner making machine. In fact they depend on it. White folks only built themselves up by standing on the backs of blacks. They always had a slave class in America and that has never stopped. The prison industrial complex is just slavery by a new name. Black people are still picking cotton for just pennies a day. One out of three black men will be incarcerated, and in 2020 that number is estimated to rise to two out of three, and why is that? That is directly related to the displacing of black people out of their community through economic genocide initiated by white America. This economic castrations by white land developers is done methodically, aggressively, and unapologetically. This is all done to help fuel what America was built off of, free labor. That's essentially what the prison business has turned into. Hardly no one says that it's actually rehabilitating. In fact, most people say they come out of prison worse than they went in because of the trauma that they receive while being in prison. Free or guilty, many people are stuck in jail simply because they cannot pay their bail. If a black person is accused of a crime and he is arrested, he may be totally innocent, but because white land developers have gentrified his community, he may be jobless and can't afford the few hundred dollars it takes to make bail. He, therefore, has to go to jail anyway, totally innocent of his crimes.

Meanwhile, do you think the police are policing white neighborhoods as aggressively as they are black communities? One would have to be out of their mind to think so. Even though it's proven that white people and black people commit about the same amount of crime, black people are convicted 5 times more than white people. That is slavery. That is genocide and most of white America ignores that every day.

Reparations are in order for all of this abuse against the black community. The brilliant Harvard Pressor Randall Robinson, in his book "The Debt" explained that reparations has never been truly paid for the atrocities and injustices by white America. In order to heal from this pain, studies show African Americans are overly deserving of nothing less than 14.2 trillion dollars. If America really wanted to be great again, they would cut the check and sign off on some land because offering tired ass apologies is not the answer.

Chapter 12: Summary

So, let's review. In Portland, folks forced black people out of the entire state for a hundred years. Any black person found within the state was whipped every 6 months. After they carved the state up like a cake for their families, they then allowed black people to enter the state to work, but many had to be out of town by sundown or their lives could be in danger.

In Baltimore, we have a historical hospital that is known for its remarkable achievements, but behind closed doors there's is a monster. A monster who does not communicate with the black residents of the area before forcing them to leave. A monster who won't hire the black people within that community. A monster who raises the rent so high, that black people can't afford to live in the area. A monster who puts up "no food stamps" signs in front stores knowing that's a major currency of many black residents there.

In New York, black people are the soul of the city. Now due to gentrification, white people are moving to Harlem and into Brooklyn in droves and they are coming there with a sense of entitlement. They are moving there calling the police for petty crimes such as loud music. The police are showing up and harassing black people which can turn out to be lethal.

In Detroit and Miami, redlining was king. White people would only issue bank loans to white families who did not live around black neighbors. The white community was able to have the power to enforce racism through the New Deal that encouraged segregation and disinvestment in black communities. Detroit and Miami both built a wall to keep their communities as white as possible.

Then in Chicago is where it begins to make sense. Crime after crime, politicians after politicians, nothing seems to change. Then you begin to follow the dollar and you realize it's the prison industry that is profiting from all this chaos. If there were no prisoners, there would be no prisons, and there would be no nation of free labor. Yes, you see the end goal of white supremacy and it's more horrific than one can imagine. Gentrification is a system that wishes to displace us and they created the hood to be a prisoner making machine. Nothing will stop them except a united front of fearless black people.

In order to combat gentrification, we must first understand what it is, and who it is helping exactly. There needs to be community organizations that are willing to ask tough questions, because being harassed off your property is not an option. Job discrimination is not an option. Over-paying for basic products is also not an option. If land developers do not want to work with the black community so that both sides win, then there does not need to be a deal done. Black people need affordable housing, better job opportunities, more access to health care, better facilities and better education and we should not have to wait for the arrival of white people to get it.

If they don't want to give us what we deserve, then we must do it for ourselves, for the best way to fight gentrification is to buy up the community before anyone does. If black people can put 20 dollars in the collection plate every Sunday, surely we can put some money together and buy a gas station. If black folks can go clubbing and get bottles and tables every other weekend, then surely we can put our money together buy a bakery and a laundromat. We can get our own grocery stores, and our own coffee shops and gentrify our communities the right way, through ownership of the land and property, not selling of the land and property. If you can get 9 other people to invest 2,000 dollars apiece every year, that's 20k a year to make a down payment on a black business. It's that simple. Build a team and execute a plan. Yes indeed, we can gentrify our own communities with our black dollars and stop white supremacy right in its tracks. What are we waiting for?